To all the kids I teach and especially to Maintenance Man Tom! - RHB

Mr. Mop and the Mountain of MUCK!

Published by Mr. Ryan's Music and Books
Seattle WA 98103

isbn # 978-0-9799166-4-9

Edited: Dan Richards
Design: Emily Booth [eboomedia.com]

Website: www.mrryansmusicandbooks.com
Email: mrryansmusicandbooks@gmail.com

Mr Mop

& the Mountain of Muck

Written, Illustrated
& Composed by:

Mr. Ryan Barber

Gabe made sure to pack his super bouncy ball.

Today the Little Wonders School kids were headed out on a field trip to see a volcano!

Sally brought her box of tissues. She has allergies. Maintenance Man Tom passed out high fives. Anton and Tammy gave Tom a big hug, because that's what best friends do.

" If you get into any trouble call this number"

Maintenance Man Tom said.

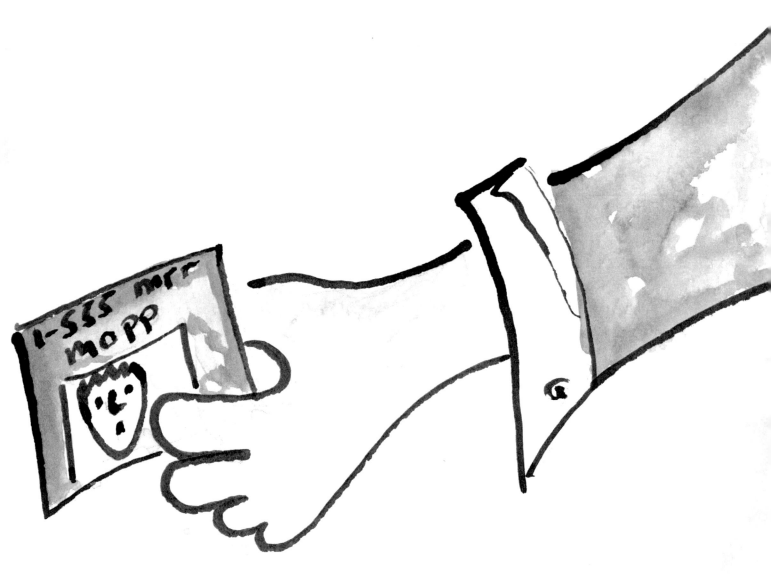

"I have a friend Mr. Mop who can help."

From the parking lot, they ran, skipped, and bounced, to the base of the volcano and started exploring the lava caves.

Inside the lava cave, Gabe saw a
man holding a pirate goldfish.

"Glub Glub! We are going to wake
up this volcano by tickling it's tummy.
Once the Mountain starts laughing
it will launch our MUCK Bubble,
and cover the entire world!"

Dirty Bubble and Glub Glub laughed
evil bad dude laughter.

Gabe whispered, "That's Dirty Bubble and his pirate goldfish Glub Glub! According to Super Hero Daily, Dirty Bubble is an evil, no good, bad dude! As a little kid no one let him play with dirt, or ever make a mess. He is the inventor of MUCK, and he plans to cover the entire world with it!"

"That's horrible," cried Tammy and Anton. Sally could barely speak, she just wiped her nose.

Gabe suddenly remembered
the number in his pocket.

"It is time we called Mr.
Mop," said Gabe.

"Mr. Who?"
said Tammy
and Anton.

Moppy
MR. MOP'S
mop - Like
dog.
MR. mop cleans
up after mess
makers polluters
and evil no -
do gooders.
He has yet
to catch
Dirty Bubble
and Glub Glub

1-555-MRR-MOPP

"Hello, Mr. Mop at your service how can I help you Gabe?"

Gabe gasped, "Mr. Mop, how did you know my name?"

"Because I'm a super hero. Let me guess, trouble with Dirty Bubble, a volcano, a MUCK bubble." said Mr. Mop.

Gabe replied, "Yes, loads of MUCK."

Suddenly Gabe felt something mop-like rub against his leg...and there, standing behind Moppy the dog, was Mr. Mop himself!

"It's working!"
cried Dirty Bubble.

A rumble sounded from inside the cave.

The Ground Shook!

Steam and Lava began to flow. The pressure
lifted a great ball of MUCK!

Gabe thought for a moment then said,
"Moppy, I need your help."

He threw his super bouncy ball high,
Moppy chased the ball and created
a doggone distraction.

Anton and Tammy ran over to the tickle machine
and gave it a huge hug. The power
of best friendship calmed the
tickle machine.

"You are too late kids!" yelled Dirty Bubble,
"My MUCK bubble already launched!"

"We are doomed!" wailed Sally, who
then passed out tissues to all the kids.

"Have no fear
Mr. Mop is here!"

Faster than foaming soap suds, Mr. Mop flew to the top of the volcano.

With a powerful push of his trusty mop, and his super hero earth friendly cleaning solution, Mr. Mop forced the MUCK bubble back into the mountain.

From deep within the volcano, the children heard Dirty Bubble yell,

"I'll get you one day Mr. Mop. Your clean days are numbered."

The children turned to thank Mr. Mop and Moppy but their super hero friends were already gone.

When they returned to school, Maintenance Man Tom was fixing a light.

"How was the field trip?" asked Tom.

"Exciting," said Gabe.

"MUCKY," snorted Sally.

"I think we are all better friends now" smiled Anton and Tammy.

"I agree," said Gabe.

"Me Too" said Maintenance Man Tom as he walked back inside to mop the school floor.

Until our next adventure...

Mr. Ryan

Ryan Barber has been a professional musician and children's music teacher for over 10 years. When he first moved to Seattle he worked as a full time pre-school teacher. During nap time he would mop the pre-school floors.

After mop time and nap time, Mr. Ryan would tell the children a Mr. Mop story. Mr. Mop is a super hero whom with the help of children, cleans up after mess-makers and polluters. Not only did Ryan write and illustrate the book but he composed and recorded music that enhances the Mr. Mop experience!

When not working with children or riding his bike, Ryan has been an Indie Rock band leader, composer, and lead singer for ten years performing in Seattle, San Francisco, and other west coast venues.

Special Thanks...

I would like to thank my family, friends and students for all their support. Creating this book has been a real community event! Special thanks William Barber, and Terre Carral.

Digital Download

With your purchase of this book you receive a four song digital download. Head over to **mrryansmusicandbooks.bandcamp.com**, Click on Buy Now...enter "0" in the Name your Price area...download and enjoy. Happy listening! If you desire a physical CD, email me at mrryansmusicandbooks@gmail.com.

Made in the USA
Middletown, DE
11 October 2015